A Calendar of Worship & Other Poems

for Bruce Birch
w/ appreciation
for enriching our
community

A Calendar of Worship & Other Poems

BY ED ZAHNISER

PLANE BUCKT PRESS
Takoma Park, Maryland

Acknowledgements
Fourth Sunday in Advent, II appeared in *Oxygen 8;* Second Sunday
of Easter in *Throw Small Bullets;* Third Sunday of Easter and
Back to Ordinary Time in *Sandscript 19;* While Angels Weep in
The Rolling Coulter; Twelfth Sunday in Pentecost in *East West;*
Ode to Laura, Sunset on Anger, What Zechariah Said, and
Thirty-second Sunday in Ordinary Time in *Bohemian Bridge;*
'And After the Fire, a Still Small Voice,' The Idol of Unexamined
Assumptions, and Remedio Farms the Sonoran Desert in *The Other
Side;* Acid Rain in *Amicus Journal;* Vasectomy in *Impetus;* A
Libation for the Sleeping Magician Death in *Public Hanging!;* and
For the Tradition and What Your Grandfather Taught Me in
ArtMag. Procedural Note appears with permission of *The Banner,*
the weekly magazine of the Christian Reformed Church.

Thanks to Zachary Barocas and Brian Price of Plane Buckt Press
and to Helen Z. Snyder, Matt Zahniser, Karen Bettacchi, and the
Shepherdstown Ministerial Association for their support and to
the *Shepherdstown Chronicle* for computer time. And thanks to
the congregation of Shepherdstown Presbyterian Church and our
pastor, Dr. Randall Tremba, for patient nurture.

Library of Congress Cataloguing-in-Publication Data
A Calendar of Worships & Other Poems / by Ed Zahniser
ISBN 0-89002-321-2 : $8.95
1. Christian poetry, American. 2. Church year—Poetry
I. Title. II. Title: Calendar of Worship & Other Poems
PS3576.A34C35 1994 811'.54—dc20 94-4338 CIP

PLANE BUCKT PRESS

P.O. Box 5713

Takoma Park, Maryland

20913

Lord, cleare thy gift, that with a constant wit
            I may but look towards thee:
Look onely; for to *love* thee, who can be,
            What angel fit?

—GEORGE HERBERT

Say that I dump my catch, shiny and silvery
As fresh sardines slapping and slipping
            on the marginal cobbles?

—EZRA POUND

He can advance no claim,
save that he studied thy Word & grew afraid,
work & fear be the basis for his terrible cry
not to forget his name.

—JOHN BERRYMAN

Contents

I.

A Calendar of Worship:
Poems from the Church Year

Proem: a Prayer for the Prophetic

Hearts go blind;
        your face falls hidden from us
by our own sweet faults.
Now every way but blank, the mind
distracts itself with endless fuss,
shut tight as a vault.

God/ess, do bend to
your cosmic crowbar.
Pry us off false pride and going it alone.
Surely the designer of apples also knew
the limits of flesh and bone?
So. . . how we doing, so far?

You can tell us.
Are we monsters, so like Frankenstein's?
(I could *never* color inside the lines!)
So. . . which of us is jealous?
Raise up a prophet; bend an ear.
One whisper cuts down hordes of fear.

Second Sunday in Advent

We declare your love again: "Friends,
    believe the Good News. . ."
with faith that it and you will come
or *are*. We're doomed toward many ends
but God/ess' love is all our dues.
The hymn tune knows: *Divinum Mysterium.*

Justin, aged eleven, stands
for baptism. He reaches the age of things
I remember from touch, not tale
or image—years spent like strands
of hair from my bald spot. Reflection stings,
and, oh, the glare! But he lets nothing stale,

not even ritual, for anyone
or thing. The scripture for his birth
allowed: "The word of the Lord was rare. . ."
Now he and Ben do first communions.
Dazed, I sit and stare
at the cross. Who knows our worth?

Comforts of the Word

W hat do you do? The morning psalm
        says: set the prisoner free,
open the blinds' eyes, lift up
those bowed down. We find our stride, calm
this week before the final Christmas frenzy
finds us circling our tails like pups.

And what will we? Isaiah
prophesies both wilderness and dry land
glad, the desert set in bloom
and cut through by a highway.
To be ransomed seems to be our plan,
with sorrow and sighing doomed.

Be patient, therefore,
counsels the apostle, James; establish
your hearts. And one thing more:
be happy. There's a Christmas wish
that promises the light of day.
We turn and take that way.

Fourth Sunday in Advent

The lesson with the children tells
how heartbeats pound, pound
in varied expectations
of magi, shepherds, angels;
how snowflakes landing would sound
like the static between radio stations.

We bet on Jesus still to take the heat
as we prepare ourselves
for the days when people beat
sharp swords into plowshares
as inventively as Santa's elves.
Let's put our shoulders to these prayers:

May all but our best passion be disturbed
this season; so, do come thou
long expected Jesus, come to see
greed, war, and lust for power curbed.
Come now
and let's be done with history.

At Worship, Christmas Eve

Christmas Eve: how faintly still
   we also lie like Bethlehem tonight
in mixed exhaustion (quite as though
we'd given birth) and praise. The thrill
almost transcends our fright
at watching angels come and go.

Drifts down from holy writ, light
on those of us who live in shadow.
A creche adorns the front church lawn,
roofed by un-Judean snow.
Why so fuzzy warm and so secure tonight?
A hymn knows: "doubt and terror are withdrawn."

Please do still for this briefest time the lies
that buttress our truce with life.
Let hunger for justice gnaw at us,
and pain for nature, that daily dies.
Angels! Come through the season's cloven skies.
Let grace abound through all the fuss.

Second Sunday After Christmas

William Turner Howard we baptize today
    to share in the priesthood of Christ.
"Tall, tuneful, and in love with the Redskins"
—the pastor prophesies his forte
as scion of Howard and Geist.
The New Year: still my hair thins

as light as snow flurries;
many vow to cut out sweets
hard on the holiday binge.
Mad shopping slows to brief scurries;
the mall falls from our daily beats.
Consumption subsides to a twinge.

A hymn proclaims "All Beautiful the March
of Days." Old visions of the cosmic God/ess
pour forth from the prophet Jeremiah.
Add to our resolve some starch
lest we close this new year manic to confess
shortcomings once again, ah!

First Sunday in Ordinary Time

Andante Tranquillo coos the organ
in decaf prelude to this Sunday mapped
as Ordinary Time. Musically slow to chide
and swift to bless, it flaunts again
the God/ess love that finds us trapped,
numb to our need to hide.

Come and listen, you who fear the Lord
(the scripture reading picks up on
implicit themes that also squeeze our hands
at funerals), be "ransomed, healed, restored."
My confidence has been up since dawn
in a quirk of the endocrine glands,

but my head clanks like dry bones
that hark back to Ezekiel.
The sermon-capping hymn intones:
"Live into hope of captives freed
from chains of fear or want or greed."
And no more business as usual.

Second Sunday in Ordinary Time

After the Sevenfold Amen
    a lilting "Alla Menuetto" postlude
soothes the sermon's earnest talk
about benign catastrophes. We don't know when,
but we will someday know a certitude
as clear as a line of blackboard chalk.

Or so it seems,
pew-bound on this Sunday morning.
However uptight, here we creep as close
to ritual as we get this side of dreams.
Bumper stickers tout their warning:
"Empty in event of rapture," a dose

of mindless certitude cramped
in brains no dinosaur would envy.
What if heaven's an airport
where Reverend Moon's disciples camp
out on your face? God/ess spare me
theology practiced as a contact sport.

The Baptism of the Lord

Isaiah taps Psalm 2
    to tint his messianic prophecy
with kingly coronation themes, in glaring
contrast through and through to
his usual agenda of justice, of mercy.
Christ melds kingly power into caring.

King or servant: both/and or
either/or? Well, both; and
sin for sin we all are saints
"Ordained for Ministry" to the world
at baptism (the sermon has us understand).
Under our bushels, lamps grow faint,

except today we do ordain
new elders and new deacons.
They serve the church by office,
but they serve the world, the pastor explains,
by baptism, just as Jesus did. Beacons
to outlandish dark: that's all of us.

Fourth Sunday in Ordinary Time

Red roses on the marble table—two today—
mark births: Tessa to Sybil and Ed;
Timothy to Melinda and Jim.
"Do not say,"
God, cajoling Jeremiah, said
"'I am only a youth,'" but told him:

"I have put my words in your mouth."
May these babes thrive
to one day speak us truth afresh.
Last week retirees flew south,
respecting winter's migrational drive.
I dream of Marrakesh

but yearn to hibernate,
except: the pastor exorcises moral slumber.
"The gospel does impugn our greed."
Nazarenes, beware how you berate
our Lord; he has your local number!"
Two roses: do stay strong, communing seed.

Second Sunday in Lent

Lent's second Sunday: we pray hard
for Bob and Harriet, Newell and Jean.
Good God/ess, we are only this community!
Outside in the neighbors' yard
raised-bed gardens hold their hope of green
though dusted white by last night's flurry.

In Genesis today a darkness dread and great
fell on Abram, not yet Abraham.
"Your descendants will be sojourners,"
You say! Abram, lately desolate
of progeny, will try the slave-girl scam:
evolution is for us slow learners.

Stroke-stricken, Bob shows signs
of bouncing back, the pastor says. News
of valiant Newell is not so good.
In Luke's stout gospel, Pharisees whine
that Christ should hide: we have empty pews
—by which we pray today, or knock on wood.

A Lenten Communion

Healey Willan's "Variations on 'St. Flavian'"
  kicks things off with lordly rolls
of organ prelude: *pneuma*, wind or
spirit baying like a pack of black-and-tan
hunting dogs. In the polls
the excess levy went bust this week before

late winter's floodtide lifted streams
to brimmermosts. Wind *and/or*
spirit ("The first, the last, beyond all thought"),
pneuma puffs the sails that drive our dreams
of resurrection—or surviving winter.
Lent hangs heavy with its oughts

and sacrifice. We dare not mention
to a soul what we give up
this private desert forty days.
Life's a two-part musical invention:
we eat the bread, then drink this cup
in unison. Believe, accept, obey.

A Lenten Intercessory

A *ria* by Bohn sets the tone, short on fuss.
The pastor says, hot on its Prelude,
"Today we'll hear God calling us
away from the rat race."
Our choice is not to pop a Qualude
but to grasp some serious grace.

Prayers of intercession for:
the parents in our church, Dan, John
(back with us today!), Anderson and
Julie, Mary Anne and David. The offer-
tory quartet says "Take Up Your Cross" in song,
and Carey, Rie, Max, and Richard land

us smoothly at the Prayer of Consecration.
The gospel reading hangs in still air:
Nicodemus was afraid to be misunderstood.
Jesus, be as gentle with our congregation
as cotton candy at the county fair
but nurture us with spirit food.

Intentional Community

Two feet of snow last night
  and yesterday—well, give or take!
Anderson presides; the pastor is snowed in.
Seventeen of us braved drifting white
(two on skis) for worship and to make
a joyful noise almost as loud as sin.

Psalm 95 punctures pride, nevertheless.
Its message crops up in the *Hebrews*
letter as an obverse call to the mind
of Christ: "they shall not enter my rest."
Mind, peace, rest: the Good News,
cushioning, drifts deep, too, driven on the wind

of spirit breath.
We draw together, exhale. Prayer
should be as rote as halting death
by taking in free air.
This week we lift up Rie;
do quell her angst for surgery.

Nun *danket alle Gott. . .*
We thank you, all of us, our God/
ess. The singing brings us calm.
"Restore our fortunes, O Lord" (a Psalmist's thought)
"like streams in the Negev." How odd
in our temperate clime, this desert Psalm.

In the gospel reading, lazy Mary
(one might say) anoints Christ's feet
while Martha tackles all the work.
Mary's largesse, rich pure nard, isn't very
convincing. We want a helpmeet
or less than indolent clerk.

Outside, the season of nesting birds
begins that time of year, the one and only,
when the male makes a show of being nice.
Communion Sunday: we trust these holy words
to thwart our great and cosmic loneli-
ness. A pint of pure nard? It broke the ice.

The Passion of Our Lord

S*ic transit gloria. . .* first Bob
  and now this Passion Sunday, Newell.
Death is life's renewing friend
who nevertheless stoops to rob
us of Your servants—acts both cruel
and merciful at this bitter end.

"My soul itself you have known of old,
my bones were never hidden from you."
Bob's friend Bruce Bowen yesterday
read that Psalms' consoling gold.
The congregation's babies chortle us through
our trebled dose of pain today.

Christ heads this week toward doom;
on Friday we celebrate his final words.
What would Bob, and what would Newell say?
We pray for faith to vanquish gloom,
faith as light as the songs of nesting birds.
Chalice and bowl stand draped in black today.

Easter Sunday

C hrist we expected back from the dead,
      but who are all these unfamiliar faces
filling up the pews we shine each week?
"Give us this *year* our daily bread,"
let us now pray, like table graces.
The curious must be granted their peek

at faith's long, drawn out mystery.
Let's see: Charlene died this week;
if you don't mind, God/ess,
we'd like her risen today
among us. She was kind and meek
in the Biblical sense, so open to profess

the newness of a thing, so teachable.
Forgive us this Easter our residue of rage
that cancer took her off so young.
Bread and juice on the communion table:
with utmost hope we turn her lovely page.
Now, let Your praise anoint each tongue.

Second Sunday of Easter

E ight days into the fifty of Easter
    we ruminate on Christ's return to life,
"now that the spectators are gone,"
the pastor jokes of empty pews. It's feast or
famine. This is feast, truth's knife
carving deftly double-edged as dawn

among believers. Recent deaths make brief
this morning's prayers of intercession
"for a suffering and battered, unfair world."
For Charlene, Newell, and Bob now gone: grief
dilutes our corporate confession.
We miss them so. Faith stands furled

and reticent today. But "Death in vain
forbids him rise," a hymn intones.
And from a coronation psalm,
"Kiss the son, lest he be angry." How explain
firm hope amidst our field of bones?
We gather to worship, in the gathering calm.

Third Sunday of Easter

A guest preacher today: John Galbreath
tells fisthand the horrors of El Salvador
—its waves of exiles, death squads
and night terrors out-horrifying even death.
Flares hung from parachutes light your door
for helicopter gunship strafings. No one nods

off to this understated pastor's voice
proclaiming our connectedness
to larger worlds. "The longer we were there
the less we knew for sure." Some choice!
U.S. guns from us or Castro via Viet Nam, a mess
that won't dissolve in springtime air

like territorial birdsong. Yesterday saw wed
Layla and Tom in calm counterpoint
to all such global stew. We showered birdseed
on their firm resolve to ward off dread
in unison. God/ess, do anoint
their love to burst all bounding need.

While Angels Weep

*S*anctus by Benoit: the organ prelude
further swells our summer-swollen air
that ceiling fans strain to separate.
Robeless, the minister avows that
"Angels weep at how we strut on Earth"
and that "Our God rules not

with an iron fist but with such love"
and "We are made in His image," so
"Are not we also loaded with that power?"
A good question. The service seems
to end without an answer.
We rise slowly from our sticky pews,

unconvincing as gods and goddesses.
Stiff knees anticipate the most
our coming benediction. A good word
hopes to hold us one more week
while angels weep; hopes to bolster us
another week while angels weep.

Organ-borne, Vivaldi's *Andante Moderato*
prelude primes us for the psalm.
It better: next Sunday brings us Pentecost.
This year we hope for tongues of flame
to stir our comfort, shake our calm,
and rouse that fevered pitch we've lost.

This morning's sermon rather
counsels calm: "Don't Just Do Something,
Stand There," a bit of lore
from Africa, via our guest minister
from a sister church out there. We sing
the morning's hymns much as before.

Prayers of intercession elude me
on this late-May morning. "E'en So,"
the anthem purrs, "Lord Jesus Quickly Come."
Admission passes for confession
—will we get a ticket or a warning?
A first offense? What, am I deaf? Or dumb?

The Day of Pentecost

Do not receive a spirit,"
says the morning's opening reading,
"that makes you slaves again to fear."
Pentecost: a spirit wind. Try to hear it
blow; sense the warmth for heeding.
It's fifty days since Easter; get in gear!

The prelude pleads: "Come Down, O Love Divine."
We've trimmed the church in red
designed for calling forth that flame.
(Perhaps if for communion we took wine. . .)
On high church days we should stay in bed
where falling short invites no public blame.

Enflaming love: today we celebrate
the church's founding, gifting burst
—onrushing *pneuma*, spirit paraclete—
of holy spirit power.
Our churches all process downtown and purse
no lips, conjoint in praise this yearly hour.

Back to Ordinary Time

Faithful sinners shining weekly pews,
    we're back to Ordinary Time again.
Advent, Christmas, Lent, Easter, Pentecost,
Trinity Sunday: all have floated their Good News
and gone this first full day of summer (rain!)
and Fathers Day—that measure of my loss

so long ago. Maria Guitz gave birth this week
to little Hector. May he someday use
the new baptismal bowl we dedicate
in memory of Newell, one of the truly meek.
Newell loved the sacraments like a muse
and left us lots to contemplate.

Baby Michael Brian William Byrne
today endures baptism's watery rite
enamored of the pastor's mustached face.
We pray about how much each soul must learn
along its path, with everlasting night
postponed again today by grace.

Sunday Three in Ordinary Time

Only be still and wait God's leisure,"
the hymnal stealthily chides.
We are fresh from last night's fireworks
for the Fourth. The sermon takes its measure
of such freedom and derides
us spiritual captives to the law. Minor clerks,

we cave in while Jezebel and Ahab
rip off again some Naboth's vineyard
(not to mention his head)
unlike Elijah who confronts their grab.
The lectionary goes down hard;
it's tough to swallow when you're dead.

Luke's gospel reads no better,
where Jesus sends out seventy two people
without a fanny pack or credit card.
Can't we just write an air-conditioned letter
or two, or raise the bucks to fix the steeple
that calls life's wounded from the churchyard?

Eighth Sunday After Pentecost

Grace Boyer preaches, from among us now,
who retired here in January.
Purple-robed, she bids us keep
the sabbath pure, despite our sacred cow
the shopping mall. Sweet purgatory!
Rest? This Sunday I crave sleep

but not before her benediction.
Leading worship, Jerry color codes
his hymnal bookmarks and chides the scheme.
If this is heaven, we face eviction,
refugees to nowhere plodding under loads
of possessions whose critique is our theme.

Ordinary Time: who can say so
and yet, who can say not?
Lois took a fall this week.
As far as our prayers go,
we lay them on her. Keep the Sabbath!
Who inherits what? The Earth. The meek.

Eleventh Sunday After Pentecost

Seize the moment; do push through
the narrow door, this morning's gospel
shouts. The window of opportunity closes,
but a demon chants "No hurry!" Untrue,
says the sermon. Strenuous efforts sell,
and best in regular, timely doses,

for "Life is a gift but not a handout."
Sarah reads a psalm that longs
for the living God. "Blessed
are those who dwell in your house"
not in tents of those who practice wrong,
or try to hide from you, as we confess.

The *Hebrews* letter's lustrous speech intones:
"You have not come to a mountain
that can be touched. . ." No. Fountain
fire rattled Moses to his bones.
Can we be touched? We wonder.
Outside, full sun, yet distant thunder.

Twelfth Sunday After Pentecost

W ho may live on your holy hill?"
the psalmist asks. You answer by extremes
—"He whose walk is blameless"—
far more subtle than *"Don't kill."*
Such persons won't be shaken. Even in dreams
we are sorely shaken. We confess!

Our morning hymns rap inner greed
and famished souls, primed by
the *Hebrews* letter's final exhortations.
By such standards we bend like reeds,
who still rebel against your love. Do I?
Confess? Rebel? (Prepare for lamentations!)

The sermon hones in on "The Lowly Path"
with "We are carefully watched at table
in this feast we call America." How true:
the grossness of our GNP exceeds its math.
We play our global Cain and Abel.
I am shaken in my rigid pew.

Wayfinding

Sing, pray; swerve not from God/ess' ways.
Now you tell us!
We follow accidental furrows for trails
mistaking years for summer days
and pick our routes by firing a blunderbuss
at ancient maps. No wonder faith derails.

The sermon heralds "Time To Change."
New mothers clutch by instinct diaper bags
and pop disgruntled babies off the breast.
If only we could rearrange
our nature and our nurture, whatever drags
these limp wills west.

And now, some nervous syndrome: smiles
flashing suddenly at random?
God/ess, has it come to this:
brief bursts of numb denial?
Here's looking at you, kid. Abandon
me not; I meant no Judas kiss.

God/ess, we are lost. Do you look
  for us? The gospel trots out
litanies of loss: a sheep, a coin, a son
called prodigal. He forsook
the wait for dad to die. He lacked self-doubt
and that DNA opposed to having fun.

"Don't Give Up," the sermon chants. "The pounding
of your heart at night just might be
heaven's hound." Ah, wisdom far too great,
too deep for small minds to be sounding.
Are such parables still *likely*
and perseverance a divine trait?

Hosea quotes you, God/ess,
whispering of the people in his ears:
"Your love is like the morning mist,
the early dew that disappears.
Therefore"—lost sheep, grasp amulets—
"I cut you in pieces with my prophets."

Dreaming the Eucharist Again

In New York City "Death is all around us,"
the principal of P.S. 30 says.
Drugs, drug wars and counterwars.
All which makes almost distant fuss
to rural refugees from mainstream ways.
We sometimes walk and do not use our cars

for errands about town.
Almost distant. . . but not quite.
Life everywhere is terminal.
Even in your love, in time, we drown
to merge but out of living sight.
We ache for the germinal;

grasp the Eucharist like an end to Lent.
Faith both sets in flight and grounds
us. Eat. Drink up
communitas: we are by sacrament
now bound beyond our bounds,
by virtue of this bread, this cup.

Approaching Equinox

Fall is grievy, brisk, John said.
   What a time to launch school years.
Today we bless each lined-up student,
hoping for two semesters of a cool head,
a shortfall of frustration's tears,
and the ghost of a chance of being prudent.

Hymn 412 praises power, love, truth, beauty,
righteousness, and grace
—on your part, God/ess. Grant them
to these students, too, so duty
alone won't stare them all year in the face.
Grant them playfulness, some whim.

Luke's gospel hammers home this fact:
we all lose things—as shepherd, woman,
father—dear to us: convictions and ideals,
our piety and passions. Leave intact
for each some inner domain
where, given your love, a deep wound heals.

Procedural Note

Communion both confuses and consoles
(O Lamb of God who takes away
the sins of the world) our minute minds.
We proclaim Christ's death, for our own souls,
until he comes again—please not today!
Yet what else in our faith so binds

us to this flesh—except *The Song
of Songs'* rich lusty praise—
as does this round of bread and wine?
Teach my soul to sing along
to the point of mystic daze.
And do not draw a rigid line

between such living life and
dying death. In both we belong
to you, as we affirm, though words go bland
repeated weekly like a jumprope song.
We wait the cup, then drink together,
souls played out on a subtle tether.

We confess again: we erred and strayed
last week. How do we miss the trail
amidst such strong community?
(*No answer,* unless that donkey brayed
reply.) In the lesson Hosea sets sail
dead-reckoned on your mercy.

The sermon aims lower: "Wise Planning"
for true riches, so we won't be
rich in things but poor in soul.
God/ess, withhold the lightning!
We confess some more, *guilty*
of being ungenerous on the whole.

"The more I called them," you confided
to Hosea, "the more they strayed from me."
So, will you keep the seas divided
for our forced march toward sanctity?
Even now we gasp for spirit breath,
this one week closer to our death.

Grace Notes

K aren enters worship in a neck brace,
   a walking, modern miracle.
Welcome back! God/ess, squelch our pride
at having interceded for such grace.
Some credit must be surgical,
but neither is joy a thing to hide.

And news from Alaska: Ross was spared
bad injury. His van flipped.
Ross works the Great Land fighting wildfire.
The pastor shouts his privilege "to declare
to you that all our sins are forgiven." Nipped
in the bud even down to the wire.

God/ess you are prodigal,
except we also mourn the highschool girl
killed in a wreck here Friday night.
Down to the wire: who said life gets dull
on a planet wildly awhirl?
Even on its dark side, keep us in your sight.

Wedding Song

L et marriage be held in honor among all;
   a holy mystery. Man and woman
we are joined, becoming one."
The pastor's on a roll
and why not, marrying Pat and Ken?
The gospel flirts with the Prodigal Son

if you know Luke's sequence.
We're talking the precious things of life
as lost sheep, coin, and son. The latter
story's title distorts its sense:
it's dad who's prodigal. Husband, wife,
we're talking the things that matter.

And here's a favorite, Pachelbel
—the Canon in D. Skills and technique
fail us, folks; hence Luke's parable.
We're talking the vision of all Israel
and of our hearts, and how we tweak
them to keep love full.

Autumnal Hints

Nights turn on a dime
    like an expensive Porsche.
Seasons roll, now Halloween
looms, beacon in this coldening time,
but where is that love designed to scorch
all the in-between?

Or is this truly twilight,
and are we on our own?
The last firefly succumbed to cold
like a predator's efficient bite.
Where is that freedom from the known
promised like a lode of gold?

Open, tired heart;
the mind will follow
like a two-wheeled garden cart,
or a dinghy while waves toss and throw
the mother ship. Or will it?
What's the secret, God/ess? Spill it.

Domesticity

From the church kitchen, animated
gossip flows. We're preparing
for someone's impending death
but can't admit it, frustrated
at this lingering on, a wearing
wondering after last breath.

No preparations will suffice.
It comes and goes, and there you are.
Or aren't. And then survivors have the needs.
Faith, whose familiarity is nice,
deserts us briefly for some far, far star.
We entertain ourselves with creeds

and other nostalgic small talk
while awaiting faith's return.
How odd, when the deep things take a walk;
such lessons you never want to learn!
Idols are illusions of control,
but death? Our only hope is to console.

Twenty-ninth Sunday in Ordinary Time

A choral reading from the kids:
      Habakkuk's obscure oracle
rivals *Revelation* at drawing blanks
and making millstones of our eyelids.
Luke pumps out a parable
reprimanding dirty pranks

and calling us to ceaseless prayer.
A widow knocks at the chief elder's door.
He is godless, a cold-hearted judge.
She knocks and knocks until he's there
for her, for justice for the poor.
So much for us; God/ess, will you budge?

We may be talking to ourselves,
and if not, neither is prayer
like quality time, or God/ess like
a vending machine or Santa's elves.
Launch your heart's desire in thin air.
(For Christmas I want a mountain bike.)

The Eyes of Your Hearts Enlightened

Having the eyes of your hearts enlightened"
Paul writes in Ephesians, on a roll
with rhetoric like a swollen stream
or dancing crystals, sunstruck diadems.
And nowhere mention of the soul
except in astral sojourn or a dream.

Must all strong feeling then be sacrificed
—so a father's actions said?
No! screams Paul; drop your former life,
"You did not so learn Christ!"
His logic dances on the pin of a head
then plunges like a death angel's knife.

Let unresolved grief lie awhile.
He wanted something pleasing to the ear
like Edmund Waller at his courtly best
or breasts inclining toward a smile
to fill the field of vision near
—the body ultimately blessed.

All Saints' Day, I

All Saints' Day: we name the dead
    who passed from us this year.
God/ess, how our ranks have closed:
Willa, Bob, Newell, Charlene, Mildred.
Communion sheds our corporate tear,
by sacrament disposed.

Neither *saint* nor *holy* means perfection,
says the pastor, rather "set apart.
We don't name the ten best saints today."
We're fellow citizens by election,
a doctrine grown inscrutable as art
but not explained away.

Prophetic Daniel dreams and asks
"who is it that will come to rule
the hearts of men and women?"
Such dreams are puzzling tasks
for this our elementary school.
All saints do graduate, and then?

All Saints' Day, II

Communion goblets nearly overflow
   but for the surface tension.
There's one law we feel
even though we may not know.
The body's surprising comprehension
rightly divides the so-called real.

The sermon, "Communion of Saints,"
plumbs history to assure us
we are they.
Confess disfigurements and taints.
God/ess does endure us.
Therefore let us pray:

a hurt and hurtful past
somewhat redeemed.
May it be for someone more—and—less
than what it so long seemed,
rich, tragic, learned, hopeful
now, from now on, musical.

What Zechariah Said

C lean and canonical, you smell so good."
   Oh, thank you. Oh, I needed that
here among doubt's horrid corridors.
We read Paul's letters and knock on wood
so our brain tissues won't go flat.
Paul's logic simulates a holy war.

Don't get me wrong.
Paul prattles on, to Thessalonica,
in words fraught with doctrine now.
(Horrors, to malign his sacred cow.)
Tell me, was his heart as hard as mica
or just awesome strong?

Let the nations know: they are but men
(and women). And you are, you are
God/ess. So. . . did we pass the quiz?
Good. Halt the wobble of our star.
We're off to see the Wiz,
and will we pass this way again?

Jesus   Theorizes   Redemption

L ife sings to itself, and
        we blush. Without story, he said,
there is no movement. I'll
tell you a story unplanned:
soon I will be dead,
and so will you. Life is terminal,

an illness singing to itself.
Sometimes we overhear a bit of it
and blush. So might you.
Something falls off a shelf
like humor from a former wit.
Many things are left to do.

Hazards of holiness linger
longer than the holiness.
So do we.
Quickly! Pick any finger.
Life flips you one for emphasis.
So, movement, your story.

Thirty-second Sunday in Ordinary Time

Oracles, night visions: Zecariah's
name means "Yahweh remembers." How
would it be to be a prophet
without the canon in your day?
—Railing against each sacred cow
but no respect. Try being a poet

instead; fewer get killed
for what they say. No,
the ultimate price is postage.
November's raw air stagnates, chilled
today. Defeated politicians show
sure signs of being reduced to stumpage.

Jesus rumors heaven,
and Sadducees bag tricks to halt his show.
Winter dawns like painful breath
here, now, capable of quelling leaven.
God/ess, we would like to *know*
what happens after death?

The Year Bows Out: a Vow

Christ the King Sunday: the last
 on our church calendar; next comes
Advent, where it all began a year ago
clothed in purple. Now whites are sashed
with regal gold; an organ prelude *thrums*
its courtly pomp arranged by Busarow.

In deference to kingship
we jump up and down a lot,
as though to truth the morning Psalm
("they'll never enter my rest"), and trip
up on Doxology, the faster tune *hut! hut!*
Pleasing kings wreaks havoc on our calm.

Last week's gospel had the world unglued.
Paul tries to piece it back together now
with "peace by the blood of his cross."
Christ's topsy-turvy kingdom wooed
us all the year unbid. Next year, we vow
all year to grieve our nagging loss.

Christ the King Sunday

We crown him King today who washed
his hands of Pilate's asking once.
Richard's mother died this week.
Oversee *that* realm, of spirits squashed
with grief unspeak-
able, whose silence skulks like a dunce

heavy, heavy on tight chests.
Help the family grieve grief gone.
So. "We seek the health and well-
being of your people," Verle prays. Guests
from Hanoi worship with us—like a dawn
after long Cold War whose heated hell

in Viet Nam shredded them
and us. Two Buddhists thanking us
for sharing worship speak like anthems
soft, precise, mellifluous.
We taste again today your sovereignty
as author of our destiny.

II.

The Idol of Unexamined Assumptions, & Other Poems

Ode to Laura

Petrarch lived "Amidst the Euganean hills"
at Arqua, close by Padua, his house

surrounded by an olive grove and vineyard.
The house still stands; one chamber

holds the chair in which he died,
his inkstand and stuffed cat

who wondered why the master mooned so
through her feeding hour.

Acid Rain

Upriver, handymen sell their houses to Strout Realty.
Eyeball enough un-plumb jambs and rolling floors,
and you can sniff apocalypse some distance off.

Here in the floodplain, sandbags sell dear.
Fishermen line their boats on rings that slide
up and down tall poles struck deep to the river's bed.

Reverend Osgood preachifies that apocalypse
is the launching pad of good theology. Even so,
they know the river's rising. They know
you'd best get yourself to higher ground.

Let them that have eyes to see, see.

The reverend tries to teach the kids to whistle up
the separate syllables of *eschatology.*
"Put it all together later," he says.
Salamanca says, no way. They think it's just
one more spitball needs ducking in this life.

Let them that have ears to hear, hear.

Letitia McBride tells Salamanca last night's winds
blew from the wrong direction. Evil, she says. They

enter your barn door and lift the whole shebang
clean off the ground. Letitia suspects
that wasn't what Malachi meant, was it, about God
flinging open heaven's windows?
Salamanca says, "Repent.
It's the tenth portion that anchors your barn."

For the Tradition

1.
Deafened by breakers
Walt Whitman faces seaward
surf-casting long lines

2.
Staring at one spot
Emily Dickinson grows
dizzy, falls over

3.
Hip, chic, suave, laid back
Anne Beattie stares at nothing
and concludes as much

What Your Grandfather Taught Me

The songs of certain woodland birds
can best be imitated if you place your lips
against the back of your hand
and pierce the silence there.

Or maybe that was the red, pine squirrel.

I have forgotten many names,
but when I hear those birds in woods
and fields, I know them even now
like characters in night dreams.

Your grandfather was my father.
He died before your birth.
He also died at my birth
as all parents do to themselves,

becoming characters in their own dreams.

'And After the Fire, a Still Small Voice'

Lao-tzu sidesaddle on a barebacked ox
blew the world's fool cool on his ascetic flute.
Half-lotus on my souped-up golden calf
I crave the best air-cushioned shocks
to soothe my worship of this lifestyle that pollutes
—Oh greed, how artful is thy craft!—

earth, air, fire and water, all the elements
and the four directions
(not to mention sky above and oceans down).
The temple fabric suffers such deep rents
our biosphere weeps acid and may drown.
Let's pray for a revival to reverse our predilections

before we sink in homemade seeps.
Gypsies are breaking camp to save their flesh.
Our Great Mother gives us dirty looks:
stress factors all-encompass her like midden heaps.
Not even scholars could screw this up in history
      books.
Hope's our safety net, if we're no smaller than its
      mesh.

Vasectomy

1.

If they had snipped the shortest little section
out of the St. Lawrence Seaway
they could have kept the lampreys
out of Lake Superior

2.

When your precious mettle
declines against the yen

3.

Within mere weeks all the fish
—to the sound of one hand clapping—
experienced the Void

The Idol of Unexamined Assumptions

Directionless, slight criticisms
blew him far off course. How he did drift:
the ruler of the kingdom of the air
could whiplash him through any snapping shift

of mood, feared fate, of point of view
or search for ever higher consciousness.
The Lord's word being rare he let no word
fall to the ground. What an emphatic mess!

Alone the brain's reportage framed his world.
He could not see outside that frame, how it might err,
but snuggled deep & deep beneath his guilt
mistaken as his Holy Comforter.

It got him other-worldly so
he was no earthly good no more.
You must not die, small you, just to the world
but also to your metaphor.

The womb's no egg recalled. What issues here
needs plunge through prayer *beyond* its brains.
Forms multiple & paradigms surpassing vast
have come & gone. And Christ, alone, remains.

Sunset on Anger

Cage the night landscape's
dead idols in dead reliquaries

at day's last service, compline.
Birdsong takes the day shift; night

work belongs to wolf howl &
the narrow terrain of oneself.

A Libation for the Sleeping Magician, Death

Our dreams are as thin as light years
and spacious as the arrow's nock
with a libretto for tortured virgins
composed by shamans and snake doctors
in the calligraphy of dancing feet
as swift as cats shaking water off their paws.

Our dreams are pockets we are afraid to look into.

Remedio Farms the Sonoran Desert

I have been thinking about this many nights now
—when I leave here and go, no more on this Earth—
that I should begin to prepare for that.

I'm working today to make a new field
and a shrine nearby. See,
my mind has been going this way
—that I should be planting things,

leaving little green things growing up.

Gathering the smoothened arroyo stones
for a shrine—*That's* how I want to be remembered
by my grandchildren—and for the live things
that will just keep growing.

Tend the Earth and help the desert yield its food—

Remedio was leaning on his shovel
looking out over the desert
talking to me as though *listening*
for the things he wanted to say
for their meaning to rise out of the desert
and come to him.